A SKY FULL OF POEMS

OTHER YEARLING BOOKS YOU WILL ENJOY:

A · SKY
FULL · OF
POEMS

EVE MERRIAM

Illustrated by Walter Gaffney-Kessell

A   YEARLING   BOOK

Published by
Dell Publishing Co., Inc.
1 Dag Hammarskjold Plaza
New York, New York 10017

The poetry in this collection first appeared in
IT DOESN'T *ALWAYS* HAVE TO RHYME,
FINDING A POEM, and OUT LOUD by Eve Merriam.

Yearling ® TM 913705, Dell Publishing Co., Inc.

ISBN: 0-440-47986-X

Printed in the United States of America

March 1986

10 9 8 7 6 5 4 3 2

CW

For Jenny and Jonathan and Josh and Teddy

CONTENTS

How to Eat a Poem

Don't be polite.
Bite in.
Pick it up with your fingers and lick the juice that
   may run down your chin.
It is ready and ripe now, whenever you are.

You do not need a knife or fork or spoon
or plate or napkin or tablecloth.

For there is no core
or stem
or rind
or pit
or seed
or skin
to throw away.

Poet's Play

Double Trouble

A scissor
and a trouser
were discussing their woes.

"Why," asked the scissor,
"do you suppose
one always has to make a pair?
It hardly seems fair
that there's never a chance to be one alone.
Always one has
to share
and *share*."

Said the trouser to the scissor,
"Yes, I acquiesce.
I'm agreed indeed!
For it's tiresome for me
to be perpetually
in a similar state of duality.
Can't I be a single pant
or a separate breech?
Instead of being half,
what joy to be an each!
Someday," said the trouser,
"I'll just let 'er rip!"

5

Flummery

"Since money talks,"
said wallet to purse,
"let's converse."

Said the coin,
"I'll rejoin."

"With no quarter given,"
said nickels and dimes.

Said sock to shoe,
"Hold your tongue."

Said sun to puddle,
"Dry up."

Said city to suburb,
"Get out of town."

Said rain to umbrella,
"Put up or shut up."

Oz.

Whoever discounts
the ounce
as one of the smallest amounts
has never met up with the ounce
that belongs to the cat family.

This jungle ounce
will jounce
you out of complacency.
If you try to trounce
this ounce,
you will be chastened hastily;
for this ounce
does more than flounce;
this ounce can bounce,
this ounce can *pounce*.

So if you meet up with an ounce,
announce yourself as a friend,
or it might be The End.

P.S. Better not take a chounce.

Having Words

Did you ever take umbrage?

If you want to take umbrage
you don't have to shake
a bottle or open a jar.
Stay still where you are.
For it isn't like taking a pill,
or taking your leave,
or taking a walk,
or taking a chance or a fall;
or taking your time,
or taking time out,
or taking a turn about.
Nor is it like taking your share or your fill
of tea and cake or a malted milkshake.

It won't make you sick,
it won't keep you well.
Well, then, what on earth is it for?
And where can an umbrage be found to take?
In a store, in a zoo, in a lake?

Is it dotted or striped?
Is it round or oblong?
Does it fly into space?
Does it have *any* face?

Is it fierce, is it tame?
Of good or ill fame?
Can you give one to me or can it be bought?
In what college might umbrage be taught?
Is it for people or plants or ants
or strictly for the birds?
Is it down in the cellar or up on a shelf?

You'll have to find out for yourself
someday when you're having words.

A Short Note

In music
a hemidemisemiquaver is
a half
of a half
of a half
of an eighth of a note
i.e.,
take note,
a 1/64th,
a fraction
whose action takes
the merest quiver of a sliver,
the fleetingest beat,
a flip, a zip, a lickety-split,
a snippet, a smidgen,
a speck, a dot,
that's what
a hemidemisemiquaver is:
a splinter, a scratch, a pinprick, a nick of time,
a taxi-meter click going
flick, snick, hemidemisemiquaver quick!

Beware, or
Be Yourself

Don't begrudge,
don't beseech,
don't besot,
don't besmirch,
don't belabor,
don't belittle,
don't befuddle,
don't befog,
don't benight,
don't belay,
don't bedizen,
don't bedeck,
don't beguile,
don't bewitch,
don't behead,
just behave!

Tittle and Jot,
Jot and Tittle

If you add a tittle
to a jot,
you still will not
have a lot,
since a tittle's just a bit,
and a jot is but a little.

Jot on top of tittle,
tittle over jot,
either way around,
it matters not.
Jot plus tittle,
tittle plus jot,
add the job lot
and what have you got?
Not a whole lot.
Still just a bit.
For tittle and jot, jot and tittle,
their allotted lot is to be little.

One, Two, Three—Gough!

To make some bread you must have dough,
Isn't that sough?

If the sky is clear all through,
Is the color of it blough?

When is the time to put your hand to the plough?
Nough!

The handle on the pump near the trough
Nearly fell ough.

Bullies sound rough and tough enough,
But you can often call their blough.

Beware of the Doggerel

A Whippet
will sip at
Pekoe teas;

a Pekingese
prefers Limburger cheese;

an Afghan
will eat a half-can
of peas;

for a Scottie
if it's hot e-
nough, a curry; for

a Terrier
a berry or
very ripe cherry;

any bite in a lunch-box found
suits the appetite of a Foxhound;

mealy ham
for a Sealyham;

while the chow for a Chow
is chow-chow. Bow-wow!

Be My Non-Valentine

I have searched my thesaurus through
to find a synonym for you;
here are some choice words that may do:

you're a hoddy-doddy, a dizzard, a ninny, a dolt,
a booby, a looby, a fribble, a gowk,
a nonny, a nizy, a nincompoop,
a churl, a scrimp, a knag, a trapes,
a lubber, a marplot, an oaf, a droil,
a mopus, a flat, a muff, a doit,
a mugwump, a dimwit, a flunky, a swab,
a bane, a murrain, a malkin, a pox,
a sloven, a slammerkin, a draggle-tail,
frumpery, scrannel, and kickshaw, too!

Why I Did Not Reign

I longed to win the spelling bee
And remembered the rule
I had learned in school:

"I before E,
Except after C."

Friend, believe me,
No one was going to deceive me.

Fiercely I practiced, the scepter I'd wield,
All others their shields in the field would yield!

Alas, before my very eyes
A weird neighbor in a beige veil
Feigning great height and weighty size
Seized the reins and ran off with the prize.

Now I no longer deign to remember that rule.
Neither
Any other either.

Advertisement
for a Divertissement

It's never too early,
it's never too late;
it's always the right time
to celebrate
any old thing and everything,
a jump or a season or a mattress spring,
something quotidian,
something obsidian,
an apogee, a perigee,
a jigamaree, a filigree,
an ibex, an apex, a portmanteau,
a charivari, a persiflage,
a quodlibet, a brouhaha,
a gaggle, a gribble, a glockenspiel,
a googol, a glottal-*stop*.

The weather is fine,
be it sun, albeit rain;
it's always the right time
to entertain
a cavil, a quibble,
a notion, a motion,
a trivet, a tippet,
a cravat, a gallus,
a quip or a frippery.

Cavort, gallivant,
escort, disport
a howdah, a nadir, a hippodrome,
an equine, a nightmare, a bridle, a grooming,
a paradox, a paradigm,
an it, a her, a they, a him,
a mishmash, a mincemeat, a gallimaufry,
a purple cow, an anyhow,
something outrageous, something indigenous,
something upholstered, something downtown,
a frontispiece, a bacchanal,
an oddity, eventually
a nonesuch, a quidnunc,
essentially
the quiddity of you and me.

Nym and Graph

A sound-alike
Is a homonym:
Sing a *hymn*,
Look at *him*.

A spell-alike
Is a homograph:
A general *staff*,
A walking *staff*.

Said Homograph to Homonym,
"Although I don't mean to be mean,
You cannot do the things I do."

Said Homonym to Homograph,
"What great scene have you ever seen?"

Said Homograph, "From my point of view
I once saw a saw saw and then a sink sink,
I saw a fly fly and a rose that rose up,
I sat down upon down,
I felt a felt hat,
And met a fair maiden at the fair;
And that's fair enough. Now I dare *you* to tell!"

"Well," said Homonym, "it's true
I can't do what you can do,
And furthermore I don't want to . . .
For I had four cents for fare for the fair,
But it didn't make sense to go in where
I'd wear a tie that was not in a knot,
So instead I watched blue smoke that blew,
And then flew straightway up the flue.
Now tell me, Homograph, can *you*
See things from *my* point of view?
For I, sir, aye, yes, I eye a dear deer,
And a hare with hair that is half of a pair
While I pare a pear beside a new gnu
And shoo a bare bear away from my shoe—
And all this I do at ten to two, too!"

Leaning on a Limerick

1.

Let the limerick form be rehoised
In New Yorkish accents well voiced:
"The thoid line is short,
And so is the fourt',
While the fi't' and the second go foist."

2.

When a limerick line starts out first,
What follows is fated, accursed:
If the third line takes tea,
The fourth must agree,
While five, two, and one pool their thirst.

3.

Assiduously I'm attending
The limerick message I'm sending;
I can get up to here,
But alas and oh dear:
Now what do I do for an ending?

4.

You've a hunger to be newly versed;
There are rhymes you would dare if you durst:
Macaroni, baloney,
Spumoni, tortoni—
But it's got to come out liverwurst.

Think Tank

Think thinktank **THINK**
get an inkling think tank
INPUT INPUT
increment increment **INPUT** increment
link the trunk line
line up the data bank
blink on the binary
don't play a prank
THINK tanktink **THINK**
don't go blank
don't leave us bleak
INPUT INPUT outflank
don't flunk out
thinktank **THINK THINK**
don't lack a link in
INPUT INPUT
don't sputter off **NO NO**
ON go on stronger
wangle an angle **GO**
thinktank **THINK**
don't put us out of luck stuck
on the brink
don't conk out
INPUT INPUT
something bungled
mangled rattled

RETHINK thinktank **RETHINK**
disentangle
unwrinkle
undo the junk **CLUNK**
plug up the **CHINK** the leak
don't peter out be fleet
be **NEAT**
we hunger for hanker for answer
print out print out print out

THANK you **THINKTANK THANKTANK THINK** you
   TANKYOU out **THINK**
REPEAT REPEAT
REPEAT
THANK YOU THINKTANK
THINK
TANK
DONE
THUNK

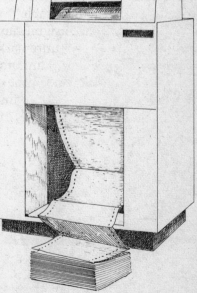

25

Floccinaucinihilipilification

Twenty-nine-letter word meaning action or habit
of estimating as worthless. It replaces
the twenty-eight-letter antidisestablishmentarianism
as the longest word in the small print
index of the Oxford Dictionary.

Why
    you
        no good
            plug nickel
             flyweight
                no account
                    throwaway
                        totally
                            disposable
                                insignificant
                                    unremarkable
                                    unnotorious
                                        unexceptional
                                        insupportably
                                            unqualifiedly
                                            lower than
                                                a hound dog
                                                    groundling.

Ping-Pong

Chitchat
wigwag
rickrack
zigzag

knickknack
gewgaw
riffraff
seesaw

crisscross
flip-flop
ding-dong
tiptop

singsong
mishmash
King Kong
      bong.

Poet's Tools

Word Bird

The quote-throated
footnoted
paginated
creature
makes a nest of
old newspaper clippings and pencil shavings
and calls out
"Encyclopedia,
Encyclopeedia,
Encyclopeeeedia!"

Some Uses for Poetry

to paint without a palette
to dance without music
to speak without speaking

to feel the strangeness between hot and cold
to feel the likeness of hot and cold
to plunge into both at the same moment

"I," Says the Poem

"I," says the poem arrogantly,
"I am a cloud,
I am a tree.

I am a city,
I am the sea,
I am a golden
Mystery."

How can it be?

A poem is written
by some someone,
someone like you,
or someone like me

who blows his nose,
who breaks shoelaces,
who hates and loves,
who loses gloves,
who eats, who weeps,
who laughs, who sleeps,

an ordinary he or she
extraordinary as you or me

whose thoughts stretch high
as clouds in the sky,

whose memories
root deep as trees,

whose feelings choke
like city smoke,

whose fears and joys in waves redound
like the ocean's tidal sound,

who daily solves a mystery:
each hour is new, what will it be?

"I," says the poem matter-of-factly,
"I am a cloud,
I am a tree.

I am a city,
I am the sea,

I am a golden
Mystery."

But, adds the poem silently,
I cannot speak until you come.
Reader, come, come with me.

A Cliché

is what we all say
when we're too lazy
to find another way

and so we say

warm as toast,
quiet as a mouse,
slow as molasses,
quick as a wink.

Think.
Is toast the warmest thing you know?
Think again, it might not be so.
Think again: it might even be snow!
Soft as lamb's wool, fleecy snow,
a lacy shawl of new-fallen snow.

Listen to that mouse go
scuttling and clawing,
nibbling and pawing.
A mouse can speak
if only a squeak.

Is a mouse the quietest thing you know?
Think again, it might not be so.
Think again: it might be a shadow.
Quiet as a shadow,
quiet as growing grass,
quiet as a pillow,
or a looking glass.

Slow as molasses,
quick as a wink.
Before you say so,
take time to think.

Slow as time passes
when you're sad and alone;
quick as an hour can go
happily on your own.

Couplet Countdown

6.
You'll find, in French, that couplet's a little word
    for two;
Voici, how little time before our couplet's
    through.

5.
Of all the forms of verse that can be shown,
The couplet is the shortest one that's known.

4.
Rain raineth and sun sunneth;
Behold how my couplet runneth
    over.

3.
One and one is or are two?
I never know: do you?

2.
Want your meter
Even neater?

1.
Terse
Verse.

Quatrain

1.
Will it rain,
Or will it not rain?
Look again;
You've got a quatrain.

2.
You don't have to rhyme
Every line's last word;
You can leave out the first
And also the third.

Onomatopoeia and
Onomatopoeia II

The rusty spigot
sputters,
utters
a splutter,
spatters a smattering of drops,
gashes wider;
slash,
splatters,
scatters,
spurts,
finally stops sputtering
and plash!
gushes rushes splashes
clear water dashes.

Therus
ty spi
    gots
        put
tersut
ters a splu
t
terspat   ters a smat   teringof
drop
    s
g'asheswider
s
 l
  a
   s
    h
spl tt
  a ers
sc er
  a t t
  u t   s
 p r s
s   fi
nally stops stut
ter
ing
and plash gushesrushessplashes
CLEAR WATER DASHES.

Markings: The Period

Left.   Right.
Left.   Right.
Absolute black.
Positive white.

Those in the know
march straight in a row.
Never a moment's hesitancy.
No raggedy baggy-kneed stragglers like me
who bumble along half-right and
not quite . . .

Markings: The Question

      ?

A scythe
flailing away
at the wandering field
of why.

Who can cut down
the mysterious grain
that rises high again
with secrets unrevealed?

Markings: The Exclamation

!

The racing flag whips out:
no second place,
no third-in-show.
Winner take all.
GO!
   !

Markings: The Comma

,

A short pause,
like waiting for the traffic light to change,
and looking at the person next to you
until the green comes on
and you move along
and he turns into a stranger once again,
the same as you.

Markings: The Semicolon

;

Diver on the board
lunges toward the edge;
hedges;
takes a deep breath;
hesitates;

        plunges.

Showers, Clearing Later in the Day

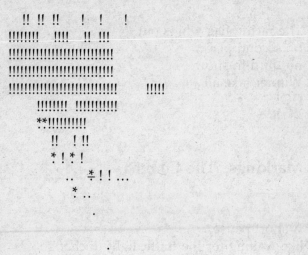

Simile: Willow and Ginkgo

The willow is like an etching,
Fine-lined against the sky.
The ginkgo is like a crude sketch,
Hardly worthy to be signed.

The willow's music is like a soprano,
Delicate and thin.
The ginkgo's tune is like a chorus
With everyone joining in.

The willow is sleek as a velvet-nosed calf;
The ginkgo is leathery as an old bull.
The willow's branches are like silken thread;
The ginkgo's like stubby rough wool.

The willow is like a nymph with streaming hair;
Wherever it grows, there is green and gold and
    fair.
The willow dips to the water,
Protected and precious, like the king's favorite
    daughter.

The ginkgo forces its way through gray concrete;
Like a city child, it grows up in the street.
Thrust against the metal sky,
Somehow it survives and even thrives.

My eyes feast upon the willow,
But my heart goes to the ginkgo.

Metaphor

Morning is
a new sheet of paper
for you to write on.

Whatever you want to say,
all day,
until night
folds it up
and files it away.

The bright words and the dark words
are gone
until dawn
and a new day
to write on.

Three Birds Flying

Once in a dream
there came to me
three birds flying
one, two, three.

The first was dark as water on a stone,

the second shone bright as sunlight on a stone,

and the third was gray as a stone, as a stone.

I rode with them
as they flew on,
but when I woke
the dream was gone.

I set it down on paper
and the words are there;
and every time I read it,
the birds are there.

A Charm for Our Time

HIGHWAY   TURNPIKE   THRUWAY   MALL
DIAL DIRECT   LONG-DISTANCE CALL
FREEZE-DRY   HIGH-FI   PAPERBACK
JET LAG   NO SAG   VENDING SNACK
MENTHOLATED SHAVING STICK
TAPE RECORDER   CAMERA CLICK
SUPERSONIC   LIFETIME SUB
DAY-GLO   DISCOUNT   CREDIT CLUB
MOTEL   KEY CHAIN   ASTRODOME
INSTAMATIC   LOTION   FOAM
ZIP CODE   BALLPOINT
—BURN BURGER BURN!—
NO DEPOSIT
NO RETURN

Urbanity

Everybody
knows
how an orange
grows
on a tree
because
you can see
the frozen-juice commercials
on teevee.

Witness

In a time like this time,
in a town like this town,
an angel flew on down.
Angel, angel, on the way!
Angel coming here today
with a flaming sword and a golden pen,
come to bring the word to the world of men.
Angel, angel, welcome in!

FIRST CITIZEN: I saw some kind of shadow pass across
the door,
but I don't open up the bolt anymore.
This neighborhood's not what it used to be,
and I don't take any chances, no not me.
My charity donations go by mail,
and I don't need a notice for any special
sale.
Don't want free samples today or any day,
they're never really free, you always have
to pay.
No. I said no. I said GO AWAY.

Angel, angel, circling round,
where is sanctuary found?

SECOND CITIZEN: I heard a funny kind of flapping noise,
but I thought it was the kids with their
bang-bang toys.
And there's all this wrecking and blasting
around,
digging up and drilling holes in the
ground.
Still, I heard some funny kind of crying
sighing sound. . . .
But there's so much traffic and horns
that blow,
cars and jets and buses and cabs on the
go;
still, I heard that funny kind of whimper
and so—
I turned up the volume on my radio.

Angel, angel, circling low,
angel, angel—no, oh, no!

THIRD CITIZEN: It happened right there in front of me,
                 came close to the accident as anyone could
                     be;
                 but it's a free country and I don't have to
                     say:
                 Play it safe and smart and walk on away.
                 I don't want to have to testify in court,
                 can't get involved, life's too short.
                 Besides, I've got a wife and two kids to
                     support.
                 Feel bad about it, but I can always pray,
                 and suppose I'd had to be somewhere
                     else today?

In a time like this time,
in a town like this town

an angel
            flew
                    on

        down.

Basic for Irresponsibility

IT is a useful word.
IT can do many things.

IT cannot shine,
the sun does that.
But IT can rain,
and IT can snow.

IT can look like trouble ahead.
IT can look like the end of nonviolence.
IT can even look like another war.
I would not want IT to happen,
and you would not want IT to happen,
but we have nothing to do with IT.

IT is not my fault
any more than IT is your fault.
IT is nobody's fault.
IT is just the way things are.

That is the way IT goes.

IT goes by itself.
We do not have to approve of IT.
We do not have to do anything at all about IT.
That is the best way for IT to grow.

Basic for Further Irresponsibility

THEY is another useful word.
You can use THEY to scare people
like on Hallowe'en.

Boo.
THEY say there's going to be a long hot summer starting
    early
and lasting all year round.
Boo, boo.
THEY say some people just don't understand law and
    order.
Boo, boo, boo.
THEY say some people have to have law and order
    pounded into them.
That's what THEY say.

I don't say so,
and you don't,
but that's what THEY say.

It's easy to play THEY.
You don't need numbers or paper or a pencil
or a ball or a net or a stand or any kind of base for support.
THEY just make it all up,
and we go along.

Neuteronomy

The elevator stops at every floor
and nobody opens and closes the door,
and nobody talks to his neighbor anymore
where the neuter computer goes *tick*,
where the neuter computer goes *click*.

You call the operator on the telephone
and say, "Help! I'm in trouble and I'm here all alone!"
and all you get back is a phony dial tone
where the neuter computer goes *clank*,
where the neuter computer goes *blank*.

There's no more teacher to be nice or mean
when you learn your lessons from a teaching machine
and plug in your prayers to the preaching machine
where the neuter computer goes *bless*,
where the neuter computer noes *yes*.

From when you are born until you are old
the facts of your life are all controlled,
put your dreams on a punch card—don't staple or fold
where the neuter computer prints *file*,
where the neuter computer prints *smile*.

There's no one to love and no one to hate,
and no more misfortune or chance or fate
in this automated obligated zero perfect state
where the neuter computer goes *think*,
where the neuter computer goes *blink*
   blink think blink think blink blink blink
     blinkthink
     thinkblink
      blink
        think
         blink

The Dirty Word

swallow it raw
    awr
      rwa
        arw
         rwa

    WAR

Fantasia

I dream
of
giving birth
to
a child
who will ask,
"Mother,
what was war?"

58

Happy New Year

Ring out the old,
Ring in the new;
Good-bye to you,
Hello to you.

Clearing a path in the snow,
an old lady wearing an African dashiki,
blue jeans,
Chinese padded jacket,
Indian moccasins.
Mother Nature
singing a song jogging along:

Wife to life,
Nurture each creature,
Breath against death,
Hold against cold.

Up and down and round go chase,
Warm yourself in the human race.

Sorrow, fortune, grace, disgrace
Run together in the human race.

Forward backward sideways face,
You just can't beat the human race.

Inner city, outer space,
Keep alive the human race.

Poet's People

Conversation with Myself

This face in the mirror
stares at me
demanding, *Who are you? What will you become?*
and taunting, *You don't even know.*
Chastened, I cringe and agree
and then
because I'm still young,
I stick out my tongue.

Miss Hepzibah

Miss Hepzibah has a mania
for stuffing unsorted miscellania
into her net reticule:

a tortoiseshell back-scratcher for her cat,
a buttonhook for a gray suede spat,
a patent leather feather to trim a hat,
a horsehair locket, a butterfly tray, a whalebone stay,
an elephant tusk, a tippet of muskrat, a tin of sassafras tea,
jelly of rose hips, lavender smelling-salts, extract of lilac,
and an excerpt of purple prose
to go with her bifocal glasses, molasses in jugs,
a moosehead umbrella stand,
witch hazel elixir, licorice whips, a taffeta headache band,
rhubarb and soda, oil of macassar, a scalloped lace doily,
a fencing foil, a motoring veil, a camisole, a farthingale,
a metronome, a wooden egg darner, a butter paddle,
    saddle soap,
a mortar and pestle, a candlestick snuffer, a chamois buffer,
a needlepoint footstool, a flannel chest liner, a little
    nightcap,
and underneath all
a lunatic-fringèd shawl.

Forever

My father tells me
that when he was a boy
he once crashed a ball
through a neighbor's window.

He does not mean to,
but he lies.

I know that aeons ago
the world was ice
and mud
and fish climbed out of the sea
to reptiles on land
to dinosaurs and mammals;

and I know also
that archeologists have found
remains of ancient times
when men and women lived in caves
and worshiped weather.

Nonetheless I know
that my father,
a grown man,
coming home at night
with work-lines in his face
and love for me hidden behind
the newspaper in his hand,
has always been so
since the world began.

Idiosyncratic

The pastimes of people
are varied and ranging:

some putter with putty
some sculpt out of soap

> some tinker with tubing
> some decorate scrimshaw

some play pinochle
some like to kibitz

> some tat at lace
> some knot macramé

some go bushwhacking
some stem and slalom

> some plan a checkmate
> some skip at hopscotch

some strum guitars
some toot kazoos

> some snorkel or scuba
> some plant rutabagas

> some build gazebos—
> all are diverse:

> for people are odder
> than anyone else.

Metaphor Man

The metaphor man
stays slim and lean,
spry and athletic,
young and keen:

exercising judgment,
he keeps on his toes,
jumps to conclusions,
follows his nose;

drives a hard bargain,
stays footloose and free,
gets hopping mad
when he's all at sea;

while running for office
he stands foursquare
and leans over backward
to be fair;

flies in a rage
although he's no bird,
and he always likes
to have the last word.

                (It's ZYZZOGETON.)

A Left-Handed Poem

HEY!
Come off it!
You're going in the
                wrong   direction
                on
                a
                one-
                way
                street
            you
        oddball
offbeat   not that we
                                                    mind,
        only can't you see
        it's
        not quite
        that is,
                not exactly   quee
r,   but   well,
                different
                from
                the
                rest
                of
                us
                here,
                    we're
                        the regular kind,
                            RIGHT?

Umbilical

You can take away my mother,
you can take away my sister,
but don't take away
my little transistor.

I can do without sunshine,
I can do without spring,
but I can't do without
my ear to that thing.

I can live without water,
in a hole in the ground,
but I can't live without
that sound that sound that sound that sOWnd.

The Measure of Man

It has been estimated that
the most medium living thing
standing
exactly halfway in between
the smallest crawling gnat
and the tallest spouting
giant blue whale
is
man.

Of course on a different scale
say
ability to create
or greater yet
annihilate
there's
nothing
halfway
about him.

Color

What is the difference
Between man and man?

White as chalk,
White as snow,
Black as night,
Black as coal;

But people are pink
Or brown or tan
Or yellow-brown-pink
Or pinkish-brown-tan.

Not much difference, I think,
Between man and man.

A Sky Full of Poems

A Spell of Weather

Begone, calm.
Come, zephyr.
Blow, breeze.
All hail, hail, cloudburst, torrent.

Grow, wind, into gust, squall, williwaw;
Spout, tempest, typhoon, gale,
Roar, tornado;
Rip, hurricane, rage, tide!

Then, spent,
Subside;
Beached. . . .

Skies clearing,
Cerulean,
Unrippled blue.

City Traffic

Green as a seedling the one lane shines,
Red ripened blooms for the opposite lines;
Emerald shoot,
Vermilion fruit.

Now amber, now champagne, now honey: go slow:
Shift, settle, then gather and sow.

Lullaby

Sh   sh   what do you wish
sh   sh   the windows are shuttered
sh   sh   a magical fish
swims out from the window and down to the river

lap   lap   the waters are lapping
sh   sh   the shore slips away
glide   glide   glide   with the current
sh   sh   the shadows are deeper

sleep   sleep   tomorrow is sure

Winter Alphabet

Bare branches of trees
brushstrokes of Chinese pictograms
marking the parchment sky.

On the ground
Queen Anne's lace brown shriveled
Egyptian hieroglyphs
waiting to be deciphered.

My breath in the air
smoke
signaling from a tepee.

End of Winter

Bare-handed reach
to catch
April's
incoming curve.
      Leap
           higher than you thought you could
              and
Hold:
      Spring,
      Solid,
      Here.

Alarm Clock

in the deep sleep forest
there were ferns
there were feathers
there was fur
and a soft ripe peach
on a branch within my

r-r-r-r-r-r-r-r-r-r-r-r-r-r-r-r-r-r-r-r-r-r-r-r-r-r-r-r-r-r-r-r-r

The Clock Ticks

get up get up
clatter a cup

spoon stir
toaster pop

stoke up
down the drain

door knob
click lock

clip clop
walk the block

books to school   read spell
wheels to work   file write

rush clack   window blind
lurch slack   lights on

hup stop   open shut
out all out   button press

clip clop   going up
walk the block   to the top

into the building
into the box

82

                   lights off
                   button press

        back inside   going down
          sun set   ground floor

        out to lunch   out of the box
       sandwich bag   clip clop

      number please   books from school
       hurry wait   wheels from work

  stamp type   rush clack
  carbon call   lurch slack

                                   hup stop
                                  out all out

                                walk the block
                                 lock unlock

                                 glass drain
                                 plate scrape

                                teevee box
                                head to bed

            tick tock
          get up get up

                        83

Ways of Winding a Watch

1.

a little forward	a little back
a little back	a little bored don't be
a little forward	you've got to keep going
a little back	back a little for
a little forward	ward a lit a back a for
	a bac kthere!

2.

long forward motions
sloop sloop like a wild ice-skater
hardly glancing back to shore at all

3.

slow
easy
before it really needs it
smug oh teacher's pet   oh mama's darling
oh put your scarf and gloves on

4.

backward first
may get there anywayz

5.
shake it   *oh you-----!*

6.
shake it tenderly   *oh, you. . . .*

7.
hit it smartly
like a butter knife clopping the top of a soft-boiled egg
in its shell cup

8.
smash it

9.
keep it at the same time always   a remembrance of this
   moment

Vacation

I am Paul Bunyan,
the sun is my bounding ball.

Leonardo,
the sun is my slapping brush.

Broncobuster,
the sun my digging heels.

Sky is my apple,
I bite into blue.

A snorting whale,
I blow out blue.

Sky is my knife,
I cut through blue.

The day is my dog,
lapping, running.

The day is my boat,
lolling, lazy.

Day is my rope,
twirling, turning.

The world is my hat
bowing from hair.

The world is my belt
warm at my waist.

The world is my key
private in pocket.

Turn key in the door
and enter once more:

I am Paul Bunyan,
the sun is my ball. . . .

Leavetaking

Vacation is over;
It's time to depart.
I must leave behind
(although it breaks my heart)

Bullfrogs in the pond,
A can of eels,
A leaky rowboat,
Abandoned car wheels;

For I'm packing only
Necessities:
A month of sunsets
And two apple trees.

The Time Is:

Do you know the hour when all opposites meet
in the blaze of up and the haze of down?

In the fire of yes and the ice of no?

In the oil of rain and the drybone wind?

In leafy will and bare branch won't?

Do you know the hour?
It is always now.

Thumbprint

On the pad of my thumb
are whorls, whirls, wheels
in a unique design:
mine alone.
What a treasure to own!
My own flesh, my own feelings.
No other, however grand or base,
can ever contain the same.
My signature,
thumbing the pages of my time.
My universe key,
my singularity.
Impress, implant,
I am myself,
of all my atom parts I am the sum.
And out of my blood and my brain
I make my own interior weather,
my own sun and rain.
Imprint my mark upon the world,
whatever I shall become.

Writing a Poem

What is there about the sight of a beat-up car, stripped, smashed, and abandoned on city street or country road? To me it seems to epitomize the destruction of our natural landscape more than any other uglification. Soda bottles and beer cans, candy wrappers, plastic containers: all the messy sticky dangerous bits that foul the landscape are blightful but manageable. You can pick up the trash and remove it. Billboards can be zoned out of areas. But the cars keep coming on, new ones turning to used the instant they're sold. The scrapped car is a mechanical elephant, a Goliath of debris, too heavy and expensive to haul away; even the junkman won't take it for free junk.

In nature, leaves rot and become compost heap; all of human nature eventually turns to dust; the metal monsters, however, rust and remain.

Thinking about them one day, I wondered if they'd ever get to cover the earth as a new vegetation. Or else, I speculated, on Doomsday when everybody and everything else is gone, the cars will be all that is left.

A poem began as a first line came to me.

What will you find at the edge of the world?

I don't know why the expression came as *edge* instead of *end*, but it did, and through almost every stage of revision I retained it. Now, looking back, I can surmise that *edge* gives more of a visual picture than the abstracted concept *end*, and considering that I was writing about automobiles, *edge* suggests a road, but at the time there was no intellectualization involved. For whatever it was worth, the phrase came as a gift.

Scribbling the line on a note pad, I began to sketch a framework more consciously. I felt I wanted a rhyme, a formal pattern to enclose the thought. What would go with *world*? I put down as an initial phrase "a feather curled" and then the following:

#1   a cave
              a cloud
                dust
                  leaf
                    voice

      guitar
             or an abandoned car?
             bottle broken?

I put this rough sketch away and came back to it about a week later. *Guitar*, I could see, was simply a rhyme for *car* and made no sense in the context. Nor did I care for *a feather curled;* it was strained, and also there just for the rhyme's sake, although the image of a single feather was something that might be kept—it seemed to connote the kind of finality I was searching for. Here is the second sketch.

#2   What will you find at the edge of the world?
        a polar icecap
                a footprint,   a feather,
        a moon flag unfurled
                  a cave   wave
        a lunar guitar
                  a seagull feather curled
            a lunar scar   a spaceship spar
                    hurled

                signs of what people left to save
                    light from a star
                        or a broken bottle and a junked car?
                    paper scraps   rusted
                                        cans

As you can see, I was not yet working with the single-
minded idea of cars as all that was left. Mainly my
consciousness was fooling around with images and rhymes
simultaneously, and like the old which-comes-first-the-
chicken-or-the-egg, I can't say. *Lunar guitar* was an effort
to make sense out of that first rhyme for *car*. I rather liked
it; reminded me of a painting by Henri Rousseau, "The
Sleeping Gypsy," which shows a figure with a stringed
instrument lying in dreamy moonlight in the desert. But I
didn't like it enough, because as you will notice, by the
third sketch, it was gone. Here I was focusing on changing
the strained image of *feather curled*, and I momentarily
changed the original phrasing of the first line.

                                        edge   earth
    #3   What will you find at the end of the world?
                a footprint,
                a feather,
                 baby gull
                a fledgling curled   leaf uncurled
                a flag unfurled

                is that what there is at the edge of the world
                    an arctic stone   cave
                                        a tree of ice
                                        an ocean cave,
                a lunar star   light from the stars
                                signals

93

                              cluster of stars
                           exploding   expanding
               message sealed in jars
               or a broken bottle and a rusted car?
                  plastic container
                a desert stretching far
                                        that
                  or do you find when you go so far
               —or a junkyard of cars?

I didn't yet have an idea of precisely how many lines
there would be, but it was a one-stanza poem, I expected.
    The next sketch was primarily an attempt to widen the
rhymes from *car* and *world*.

                                        rim
                                        edge
    #4   What will you find at the end of the world?
                                    horizon's end
               A footprint,
                a feather,
                a flag unfurled?   a cave of ice
               Is that what there is at the edge of the world?
         ghostly silence   a single tree, the wind blowing free
                                            explored
                                            toward
                 Or do you find when you go that far
                           a cluster   blaze   manmade stars
               a cavern reflecting light from the stars
               or a junkyard of cars?

I tried to pull things together and wrote out this:

    #5   What will you find at the edge of the world?
           A footprint,

                              94

           a plastic container
           and a rusted car?
      a single pebble
   bubble in sand   roar of the sea
   a shell   sandbar— a lunar landscape
                    metallic fin
   a door left ajar   a leaf   a stone
           a single flower in a field
              buried gold   a prowling cat
                 a perfect bubble
              creature unknown

In this version I was putting down whatever images
came to mind that would convey isolation, the end of
human civilization. Clichés were studded throughout the
scribbled phrases, but I wasn't stopping to censor myself
at this stage. (Incidentally, I later realized that A Single
Pebble had been used as the title of a novel, and A Leaf,
A Stone, A Door came from Thomas Wolfe.) *Buried gold,
the roar of the sea, wind blowing free, ghostly silence:* these
were almost perfect examples of the banal, but I went on
anyway. The next sketch went back to the original: *What
will you find at the edge of the world?* Now I felt on firm
footing: no more changes in that opening: if I lost it, I'd
lose the poem.

   #5A   A footprint,
            a feather,
            by the wind whorled   gnarled   snarled
               a leaf uncurled,
            a sea cave   engulfing darkness
                          snowfall
                          a feather,
                          a leaf uncurled,
                          a cave of ice,

             a cluster of stars
             or a junkyard of cars?

From that, a second stanza began to evolve and I felt a
new rush of excitement as the poem was taking shape.
Bottles and containers were out; the car image would be
focused on doubly.

    #5B   What will there be at the rim of the earth?

               A perfect bubble,
               a single tree,
               a miracle birth?
               the roar of the sea
               the silence of planets stars
               —or the traffic of cars?

When I read it over, the idea of traffic still moving and
noise at world's end struck me as wrong. So a variation
emerged for the second stanza.

    #6   What will there be at the rim of the earth
                                      outermost rim
                                        horizon dim
               lightning
               thunder
                 baby lamb's
               a new creature's birth
               horizons blazing   unending sunrise
                               a sea cave deep   steep
                                   sleep
                               immortal sleep   creep
               or cars piled up in a rusty heap.

                              96

The end now seemed right, and getting rid of the cliché of *miracle birth* helped. I went back to work on what was now stanza one.

#7   What will you find at the edge of the world?
      A footprint,
      a feather,
          seedling curled   lightning hurled
      a leaf uncurled
          single leaf curled
      engulfing darkness
      exploding stars
      a rainfall
                  rainbow
                  snowfall of stars

The final line of that stanza, *or a junkyard of cars*, was fixed, I felt, but the rhyme for *world* was still giving me trouble. I didn't like any of the images; they seemed stale *(lightning hurled)* or awkward *(seedling curled)*. Curled in what? I could justify its use if I had to—the embryonic shape curled up into a ball—but rationalization was not going to complete the poem.

My next version, therefore, concentrated on trying to get a new *world* rhyme/image. I tried a white sheet of paper instead of lined yellow ledger sheets; maybe the snowy blankness would lead to fresh ideas? No luck. I even used a rhyming dictionary—something I rarely do. *Furled, twirled, swirled, whirled, skirled. Ocean waves whirled?* I realized by now this was an identical rhyme: so much for the dictionary's help! *Strange music skirled? A thunderbolt hurled? Desert sand swirled?* Discouraged, I went back to *a leaf uncurled* and put the poem aside.

A few days later I typed it out cleanly.

#7A What will you find at the edge of the world?
      A footprint,
      a feather,
      a seedling curled?
      Unending sunrise,
      immortal sleep,
      or cars piled up in a rusty heap?

The last three lines, like the first three, remained as they
had been. *Rain of stars* was better than the three other
choices, and I would settle for that. Still, *thunderbolt hurled*
was no more satisfactory to me in the long run than
seedling curled. At this point I became aware that if I
continued to worry it, the poem would only deteriorate.
Put it aside was self's advice to self.

Then, a month later, I was on a lecture trip in the
Midwest. At night, in my hotel room, I thought over the
poem again and wrote it down from memory. Immediately
after I did, I crossed out the offending thunderbolt and
wrote in *desert sand swirled*, elated that I had found a new
image and completely unaware that it was one I had
considered earlier. But using it brought the old problem
of similar images. If there was desert sand in the first
stanza, it would be impossible to have a sand dune in the
second. How about instead of *sand dune* the word *canyon*?
Or *sea cave*? Or *grass*, or *prairie*? *Coral reef*? A two-syllable
phrase was needed to maintain the rhythm; *grass* and
coral reef were eliminated. *Prairie* was not stripped bare
enough for world's end. It would have to be *canyon*. Now
the phrasing went:

      a crater,
      a canyon,
      a new creature's birth.

Without even consciously saying to myself: *Too pat, too
alliterative with all those hard* c *sounds,* there suddenly jumped
into my mind this sequence:

> Engulfing darkness,
> a rainbow of stars,
> or a junkyard of cars?
>
> What will there be at the rim of the earth?
> Lightning,
> thunder,
> a new creature's birth?
> Unending sunrise,
> immortal sleep,
> or cars piled up in a rusty heap?

The fourth line of the first stanza was still a stopper to me.
What if I substituted *thunderbolt hurled*? Then I'd have to
take thunder out of the second stanza. And if I did, *engulfing
darkness* and *a rainbow of stars* ought also to be dropped;
they were too close in imagery to the thunderbolt.

So now it read:

> #8   What will you find at the edge of the world?
> A footprint,
> a feather,
> a thunderbolt hurled?
> A tree of ice,
>   snowfall   crown
> a garden
>   rain of stars,
> or a junkyard of cars?

What will there be at the rim of the earth?
A sand dune,
a crater,
a new creature's birth?

a mollusc,
a mammal,
a new creature's birth?

The sequence seemed right, and when I wrote it out it still seemed fitting. So here now is the poem. I'm still not altogether pleased; *desert sand swirled* is a little too sibilant to read aloud easily. Perhaps someday I'll find another image,* but for now I'm satisfied that the poem is what I want to say in the way I have found to say it.

* or perhaps you will

Landscape

What will you find at the edge of the world?
A footprint,
a feather,
desert sand swirled?
A tree of ice,
a rain of stars,
or a junkyard of cars?

What will there be at the rim of the earth?
A mollusc,
a mammal,
a new creature's birth?
Eternal sunrise,
immortal sleep,
or cars piled up in a rusty heap?